W9-BWT-827

San Francisco 49ers

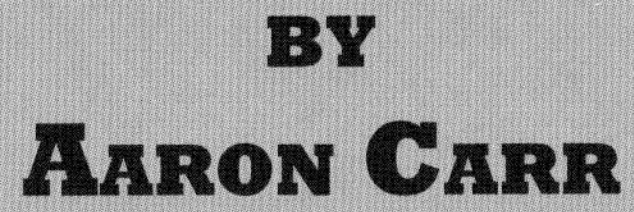

BY

Aaron Carr

www.av2books.com

Go to www.av2books.com, and enter this book's unique code.

BOOK CODE

R858879

AV² by Weigl brings you media enhanced books that support active learning.

AV² provides enriched content that supplements and complements this book. Weigl's AV² books strive to create inspired learning and engage young minds in a total learning experience.

Your AV² Media Enhanced books come alive with...

Audio
Listen to sections of the book read aloud.

Key Words
Study vocabulary, and complete a matching word activity.

Video
Watch informative video clips.

Quizzes
Test your knowledge.

Embedded Weblinks
Gain additional information for research.

Slide Show
View images and captions, and prepare a presentation.

Try This!
Complete activities and hands-on experiments.

... and much, much more!

Published by AV² by Weigl
350 5th Avenue, 59th Floor
New York, NY 10118
Websites: www.av2books.com www.weigl.com

Library of Congress Control Number: 2014930838

ISBN 978-1-4896-0886-4 (hardcover)
ISBN 978-1-4896-0888-8 (single-user eBook)
ISBN 978-1-4896-0889-5 (multi-user eBook)

Printed in the United States of America in North Mankato, Minnesota
1 2 3 4 5 6 7 8 9 0 18 17 16 15 14

042014
WEP150314

Senior Editor Aaron Carr
Art Director Terry Paulhus

Photo Credits
Every reasonable effort has been made to trace ownership and to obtain permission to reprint copyright material. The publishers would be pleased to have any errors or omissions brought to their attention so that they may be corrected in subsequent printings.

Weigl acknowledges Getty Images as its primary image supplier for this title.

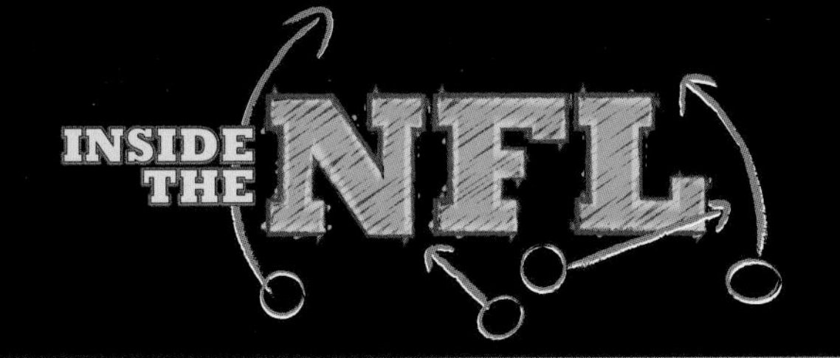

San Francisco 49ers

CONTENTS

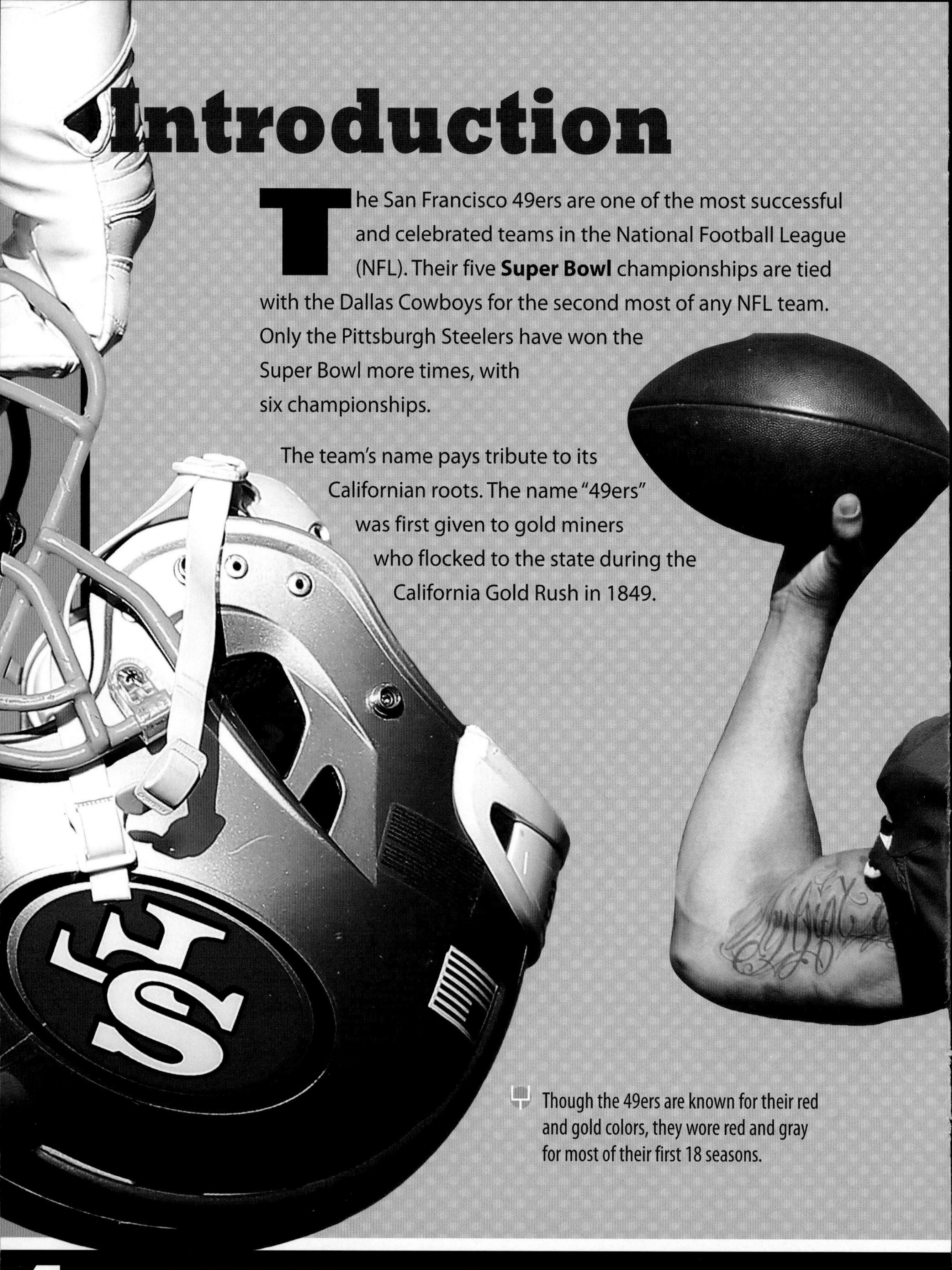

Introduction

The San Francisco 49ers are one of the most successful and celebrated teams in the National Football League (NFL). Their five **Super Bowl** championships are tied with the Dallas Cowboys for the second most of any NFL team. Only the Pittsburgh Steelers have won the Super Bowl more times, with six championships.

The team's name pays tribute to its Californian roots. The name "49ers" was first given to gold miners who flocked to the state during the California Gold Rush in 1849.

Though the 49ers are known for their red and gold colors, they wore red and gray for most of their first 18 seasons.

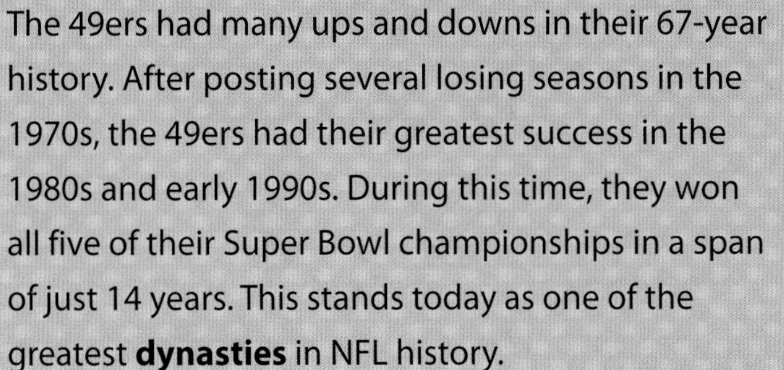

The 49ers had many ups and downs in their 67-year history. After posting several losing seasons in the 1970s, the 49ers had their greatest success in the 1980s and early 1990s. During this time, they won all five of their Super Bowl championships in a span of just 14 years. This stands today as one of the greatest **dynasties** in NFL history.

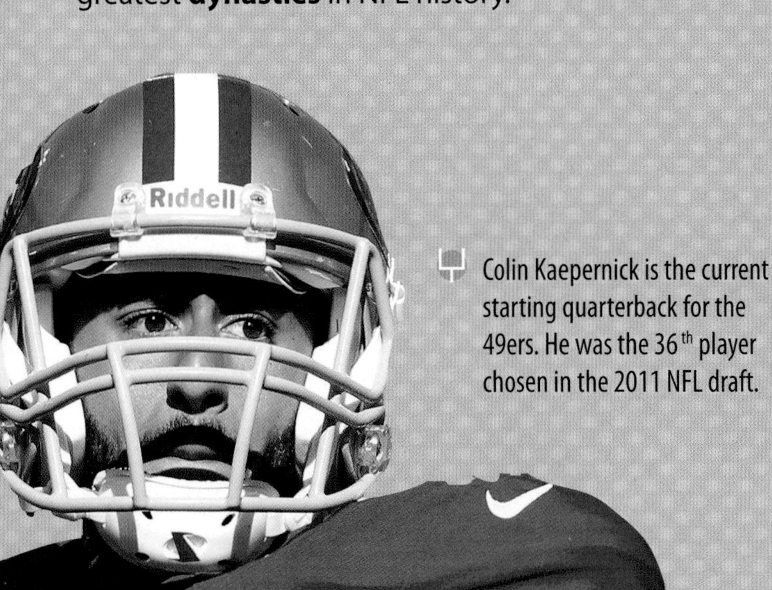

Colin Kaepernick is the current starting quarterback for the 49ers. He was the 36th player chosen in the 2011 NFL draft.

San Francisco 49ers

Stadium Levi's Stadium

Division National Football Conference (NFC) West

Head Coach Jim Harbaugh

Location San Francisco area

Super Bowl Championships 1981, 1984, 1988, 1989, 1994

Nicknames The Niners, The Gold Rush, The Red and Gold, Bay Bombers

26 Playoff Appearances

5 Super Bowl Championships

19 Division Championships

History

22
49ers have been inducted into the Pro Football Hall of Fame

Joe Montana holds the distinction of never throwing an interception in a Super Bowl game. He attempted 122 passes through four Super Bowls, completing 83 of them.

In the mid-1940s, San Francisco was a thriving city. There were no professional sports teams in California at this time, but college football was attracting huge crowds across the state. Tony Morabito, the owner of a lumber company, decided San Francisco would be the perfect place for the NFL to expand with a new team. The NFL did not agree with Morabito, however, and turned down his request for a team.

In 1946, a new professional football league was founded. The San Francisco 49ers became one of the first teams to join the **All-American** Football Conference (AAFC). The 49ers played four seasons in the AAFC before the league became a part of the NFL. The team played its first NFL season in 1950.

The team enjoyed only moderate success during its first 30 years in the NFL. The 49ers had first-place finishes in the 1970, 1971, and 1972 seasons but could not continue that success in the playoffs. That all changed in 1981. With a new coaching staff and rising stars, such as Joe Montana and Ronnie Lott, the 49ers kicked off a 16-year streak of dominance. Over that period, the team finished in first place 12 times.

Jerry Rice scored 1,256 points in his career. Not counting kickers, this makes Rice the highest scoring player in NFL history.

The Stadium

Levi's Stadium will seat about 68,500 people for football games.

From the team's first season in the AAFC until the end of the 1970 NFL season, the San Francisco 49ers called Kezar Stadium home. The stadium opened in 1925 and seated just under 60,000 people. The last game at Kezar Stadium took place on January 3, 1971, when the 49ers lost to the Dallas Cowboys 17-10 in the NFC Championship.

The San Francisco fans are known as the 49ers Faithful. They often travel to support their team in away games.

From 1971 to 2013, the 49ers played in Candlestick Park. Opened in 1960, Candlestick Park is an outdoor stadium that seats nearly 70,000 fans. From 1960 to 1999, Candlestick Park was also home to the San Francisco Giants Major League Baseball team.

In 2006, the 49ers began looking for a place to build a new stadium. The owners decided to build in the nearby city of Santa Clara. Construction began on the new Levi's Stadium in 2012. It is scheduled to open in time for the start of the 2014 NFL season. The new stadium is slotted to host the Super Bowl in 2016.

The 49ers franchise makes $6.8 million per year on concession and merchandise sales. Restaurants such as the Gridiron Grill are very popular among local fans.

Where They Play

AMERICAN FOOTBALL CONFERENCE

EAST	NORTH	SOUTH	WEST
1 Gillette Stadium	5 FirstEnergy Stadium	9 EverBank Field	13 Arrowhead Stadium
2 MetLife Stadium	6 Heinz Field	10 LP Field	14 Sports Authority Field at Mile High
3 Ralph Wilson Stadium	7 M&T Bank Stadium	11 Lucas Oil Stadium	15 O.co Coliseum
4 Sun Life Stadium	8 Paul Brown Stadium	12 NRG Stadium	16 Qualcomm Stadium

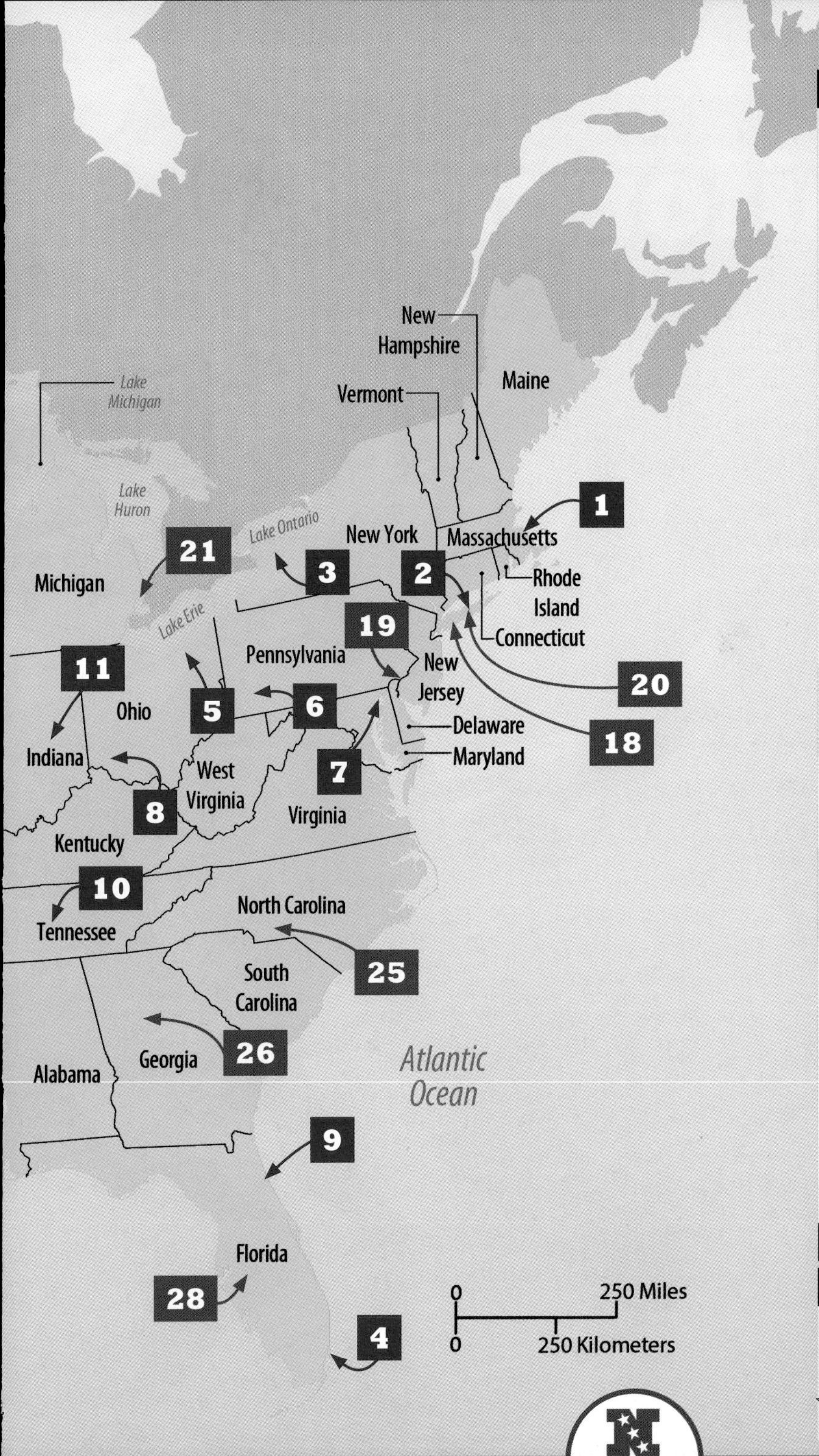

Levi's® STADIUM

Location
4900 Centennial Boulevard
Santa Clara, CA

Broke ground
April 19, 2012

Completed
Summer 2014

Surface
Natural grass

Features
- green roof with solar panels
- stadium-wide Wi-Fi
- 13,600 square feet (1,263 square meters) of HD screens
- year-round commercial and community space
- the 49ers Hall of Fame

LEGEND
- American Football Conference
- National Football Conference
- ☆ Levi's Stadium

NATIONAL FOOTBALL CONFERENCE

EAST	NORTH	SOUTH	WEST
17 AT&T Stadium	21 Ford Field	25 Bank of America Stadium	★ 29 Levi's Stadium
18 FedExField	22 Lambeau Field	26 Georgia Dome	30 CenturyLink Field
19 Lincoln Financial Field	23 Mall of America Field	27 Mercedes-Benz Superdome	31 Edward Jones Dome
20 MetLife Stadium	24 Soldier Field	28 Raymond James Stadium	32 University of Phoenix Stadium

The Uniforms

12 Number of jerseys the San Francisco 49ers have retired

Though other parts of the 49ers' uniform have changed, the primary colors of red for home and white for away have always stayed the same.

The 49ers' team colors are red, gold, and white. Though the uniform design has changed many times over the years, the colors have remained largely unchanged since 1964.

HOME

Today, the 49ers' home jersey is red with white stripes and lettering. The pants are gold with red and white stripes down the outsides of the legs, and the socks are white on the lower half and red on the upper half. The jersey does not have a **logo**. Instead, it has the word "49ers" in white text across the front.

The away uniform is the same except for the jersey. For away games, the 49ers wear white jerseys with red stripes and lettering.

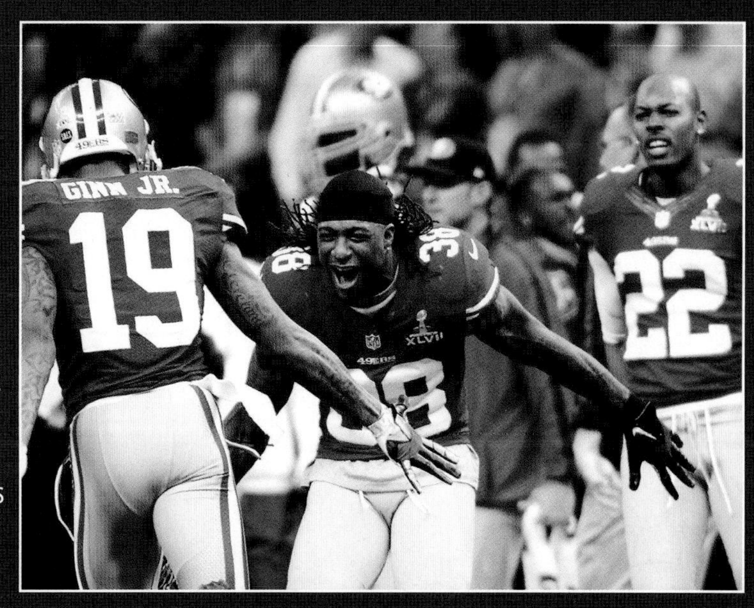

NFL uniforms are made to fit snugly to the player's body. This ensures there is no extra material for opposing players to grab and hold on to.

The Helmets

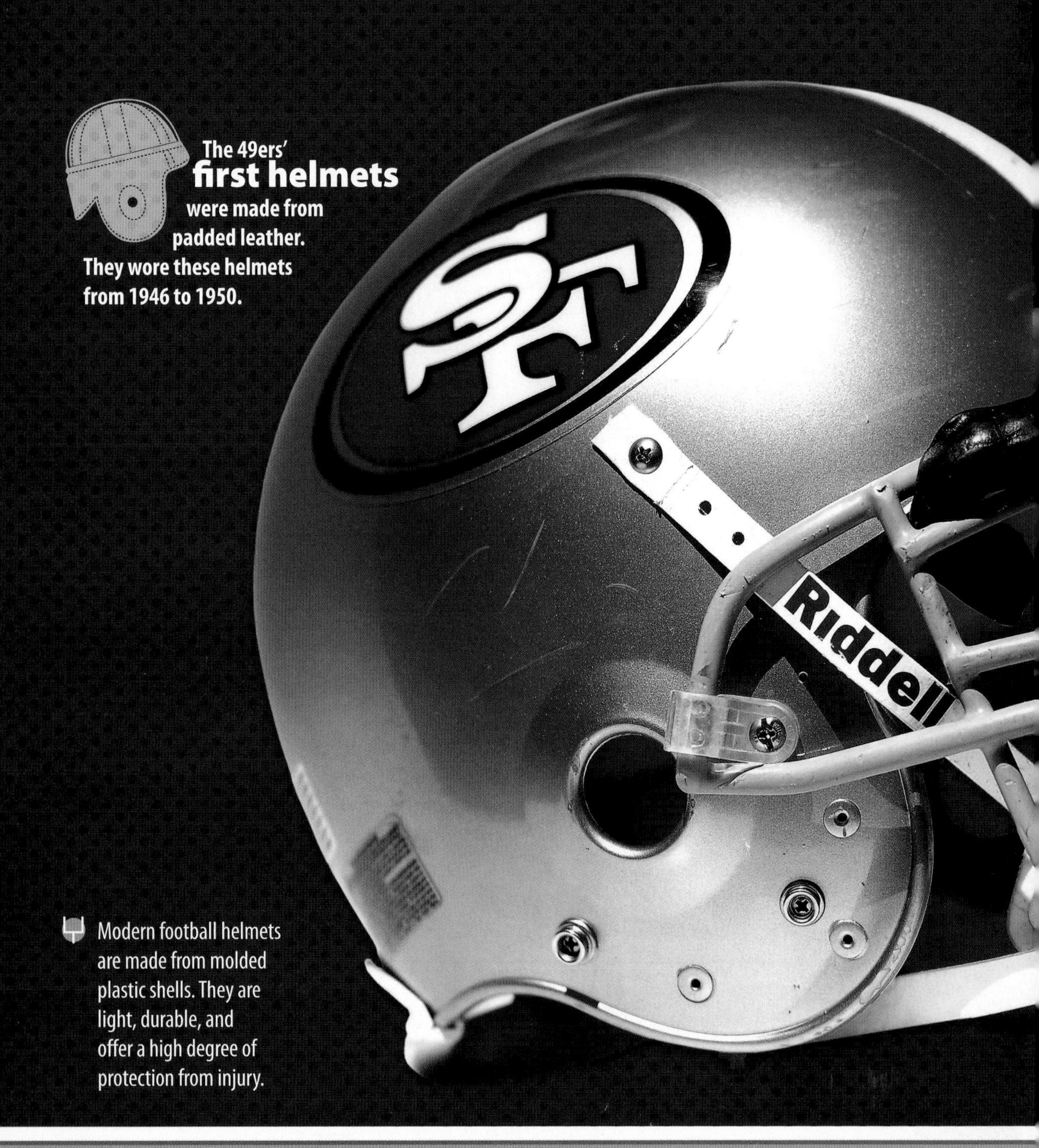

The 49ers' **first helmets** were made from padded leather. They wore these helmets from 1946 to 1950.

Modern football helmets are made from molded plastic shells. They are light, durable, and offer a high degree of protection from injury.

The color and design of the 49ers' helmet has changed many times since the team first took the field. Early 49ers' helmet designs included the red helmets of the early 1950s, the gold helmet with no stripes worn from 1957 to 1958, and the 1962 to 1963 silver helmet with red and white stripes. The 1962 helmet was the first 49ers' helmet to include the team logo. Through the years, the main color of the helmet has most often been gold.

The current 49ers' helmet is gold with a wide white stripe running down the center of the helmet. There is a thinner red stripe on either side of the white stripe. Both sides of the helmet show the 49ers' team logo. The logo shows the letters 'S' and 'F' overlapping each other inside a football-shaped oval. The oval is filled with 49ers' red and has black and gold trim.

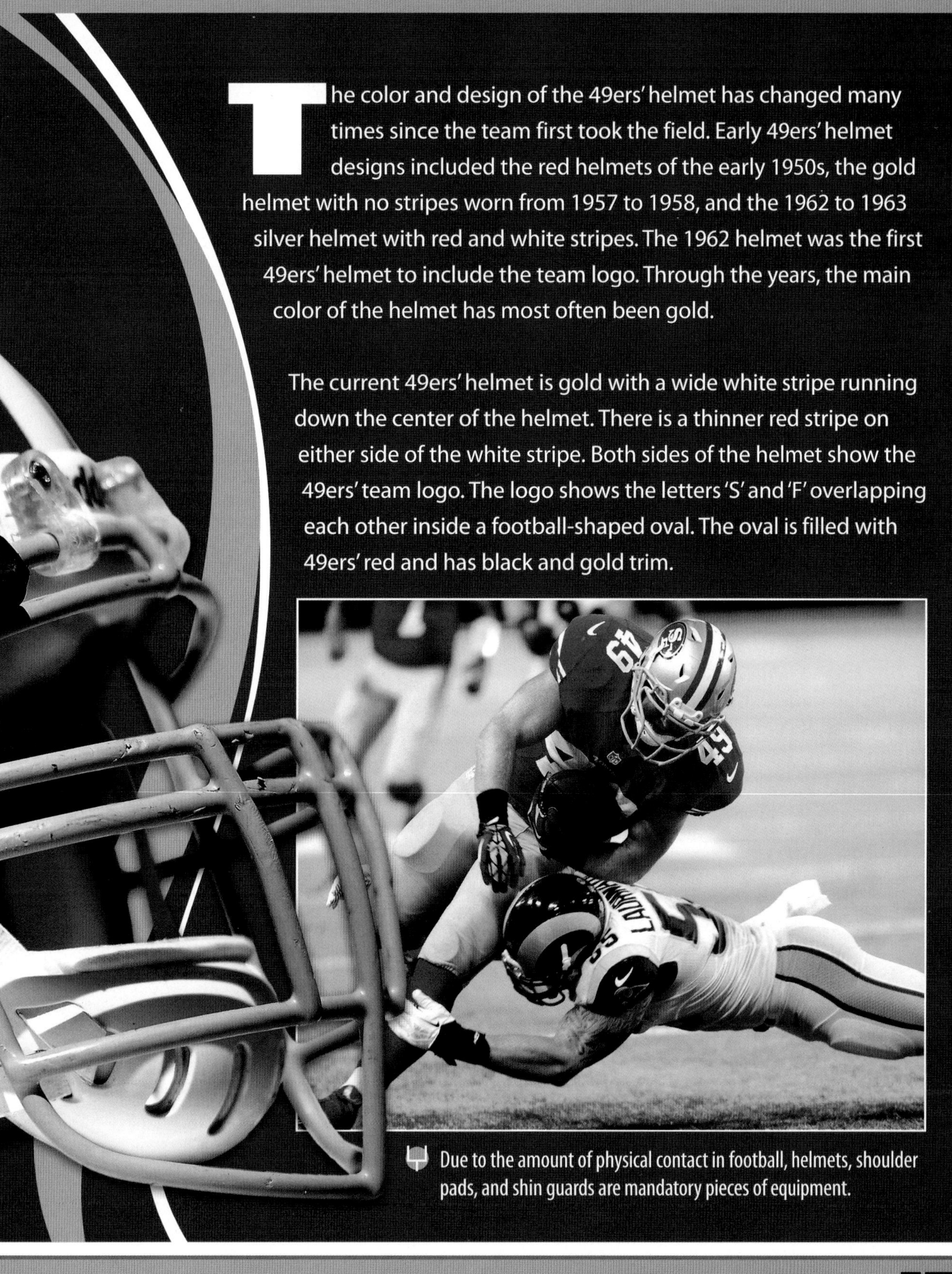

Due to the amount of physical contact in football, helmets, shoulder pads, and shin guards are mandatory pieces of equipment.

The Coaches

1 The number of times in NFL history that two brothers have squared off in the Super Bowl.

In Super Bowl XLVII, coach Jim Harbaugh led the San Francisco 49ers against his brother John Harbaugh, who coached the Baltimore Ravens. The Ravens won 34-31.

Jim Harbaugh is often compared to 49ers great Bill Walsh because of his coaching style. Both coaches built their teams on organization and accountability.

The 49ers' success over the past 30 years is partly due to the coaches who have led the team. Legendary coach Bill Walsh helped turn the 49ers into a dynasty in the 1980s. George Seifert took over for Walsh and continued the team's success into the mid-1990s. After nearly a decade of poor results, Jim Harbaugh took over coaching duties and led the 49ers back to the top of the NFL.

BILL WALSH

Bill Walsh became head coach of the 49ers in 1979. After winning just two games in his first season, he led the 49ers through one of the most successful periods of its history. He is known for his West Coast offense. He was inducted into the Pro Sports Hall of Fame in 1993.

GEORGE SEIFERT

George Seifert was the 49ers' defensive coordinator when Bill Walsh retired. Seifert then took over as head coach. He led the 49ers to two Super Bowl victories. Seifert posted more wins and a higher **winning percentage** than any other 49ers coach.

JIM HARBAUGH

Jim Harbaugh became the 49ers' head coach in 2011. At this time, the 49ers had not made it to the playoffs in eight years. In his first year with the team, Harbaugh led the 49ers to the NFC championship game. Next year, he led the team to a Super Bowl appearance. In his first three seasons as coach, the 49ers posted a 36-11-1 win-loss-tie record.

The Mascot

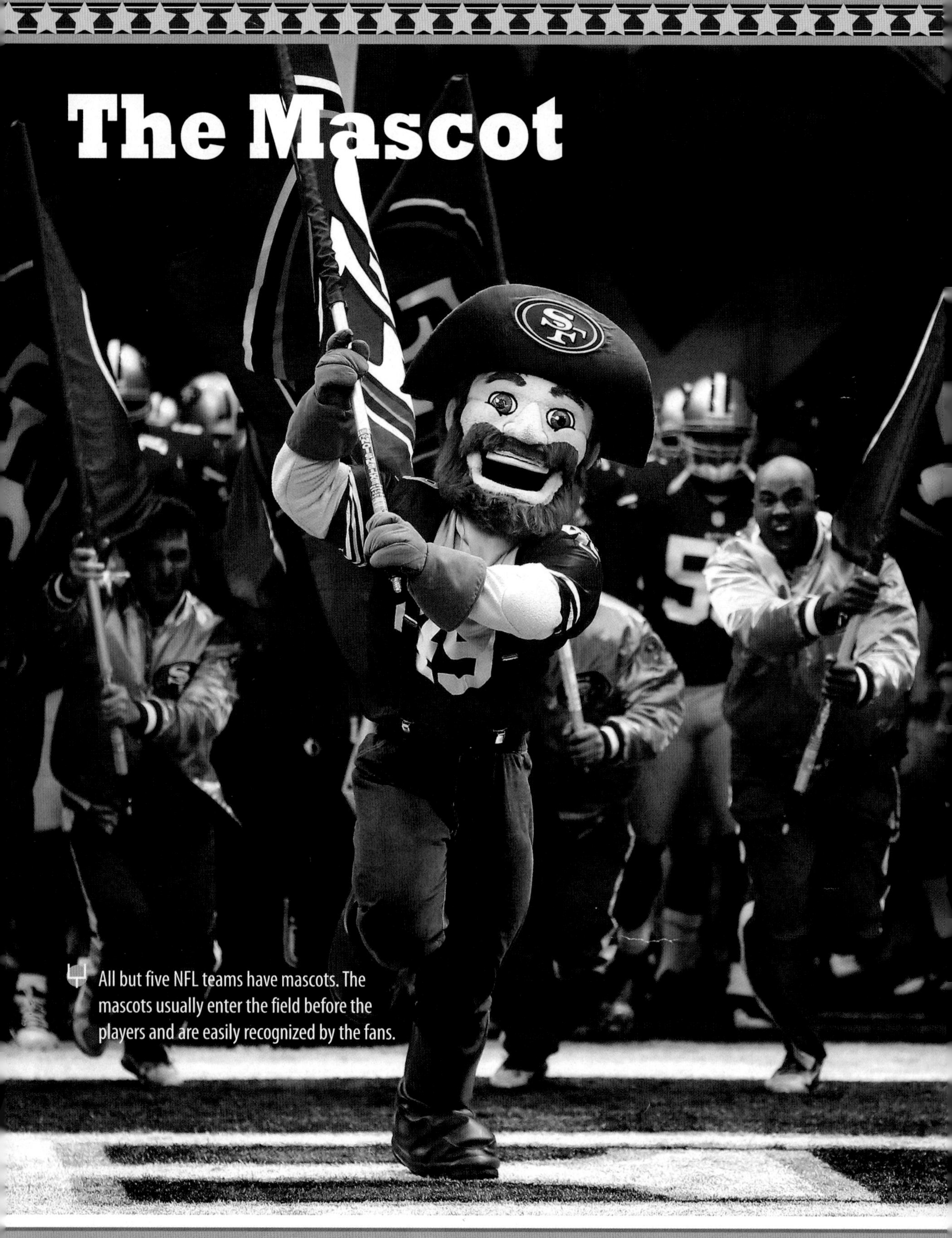

All but five NFL teams have mascots. The mascots usually enter the field before the players and are easily recognized by the fans.

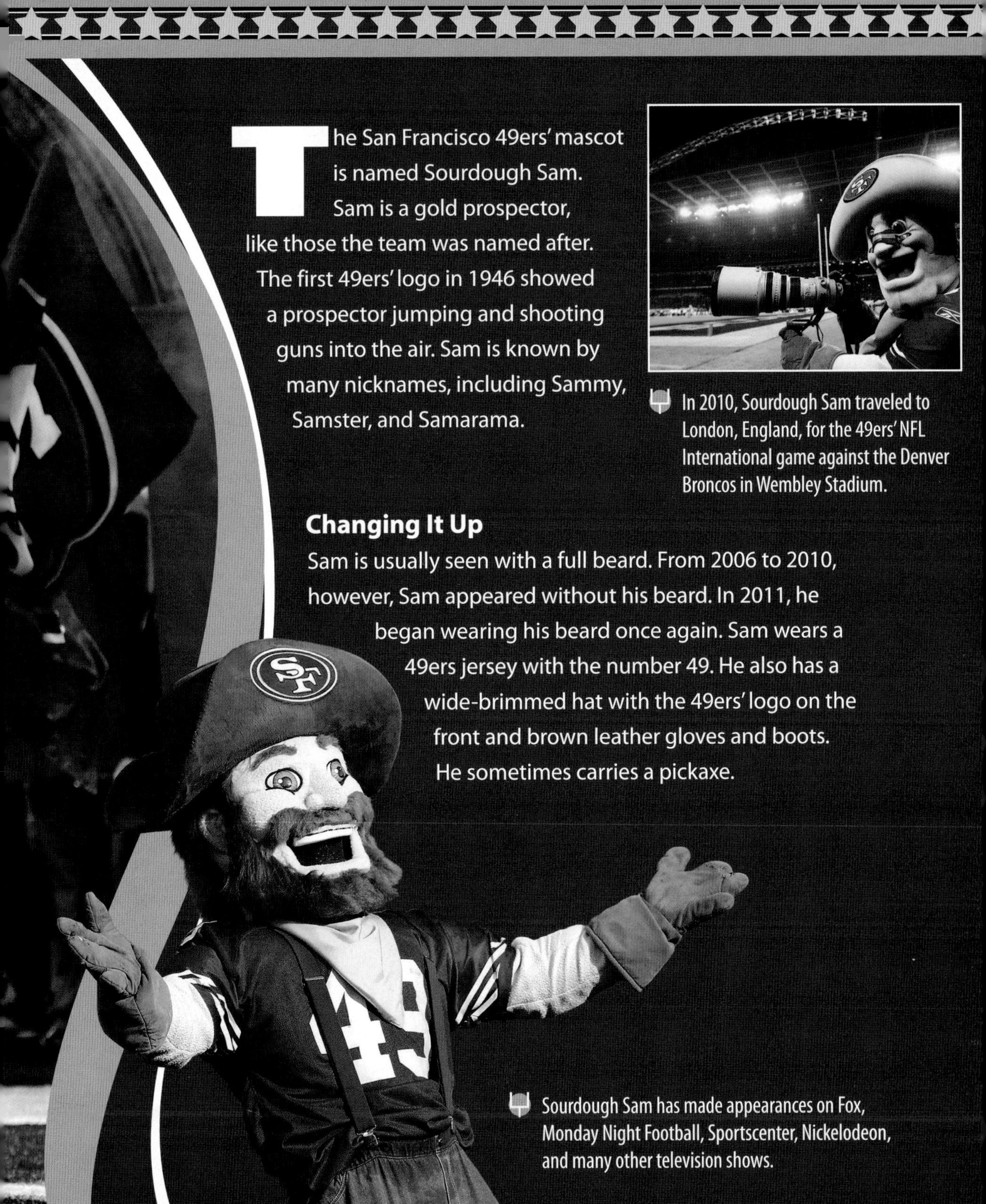

The San Francisco 49ers' mascot is named Sourdough Sam. Sam is a gold prospector, like those the team was named after. The first 49ers' logo in 1946 showed a prospector jumping and shooting guns into the air. Sam is known by many nicknames, including Sammy, Samster, and Samarama.

In 2010, Sourdough Sam traveled to London, England, for the 49ers' NFL International game against the Denver Broncos in Wembley Stadium.

Changing It Up

Sam is usually seen with a full beard. From 2006 to 2010, however, Sam appeared without his beard. In 2011, he began wearing his beard once again. Sam wears a 49ers jersey with the number 49. He also has a wide-brimmed hat with the 49ers' logo on the front and brown leather gloves and boots. He sometimes carries a pickaxe.

Sourdough Sam has made appearances on Fox, Monday Night Football, Sportscenter, Nickelodeon, and many other television shows.

Legends of the Past

Many great players have suited up in 49ers' red and gold. A few of them have become icons of the team and the city it represents.

Joe Montana

Position Quarterback
NFL Seasons 16 (1979–1994)
Born June 11, 1956, in New Eagle, Pennsylvania

Joe Montana is thought to be one of the greatest quarterbacks of all time. He was best known for his ability to stay calm under pressure. This earned him the nickname "Joe Cool." Montana was at his best in big games. He played in four Super Bowls and won them all. He was named the **most valuable player (MVP)** of the Super Bowl three times. Montana was inducted into the Pro Football Hall of Fame in 2000.

Jerry Rice

When he retired, Jerry Rice held nearly every record for a wide receiver, including receptions, touchdowns, and yards. He is considered the greatest wide receiver ever to play the game. In 2010, the NFL Network voted Rice the greatest player in NFL history. Rice won three Super Bowl championships with the 49ers, and he was named MVP of Super Bowl XXIII. He was inducted into the Pro Football Hall of Fame in 2010.

Position Wide Receiver
Seasons 20 (1985–2004)
Born October 13, 1962, in Starkville, Mississippi

Leo Nomellini

Leo Nomellini became the 49ers' first ever draft pick in 1950. Though he had only started playing football eight years earlier, Nomellini proved his skills as a two-time All-American at the University of Minnesota.

In the NFL, Nomellini played his entire career in San Francisco. He did not miss a single game in 14 years with the 49ers while playing both defensive and offensive tackle. Nomellini was named an **All-Pro** at both positions. He was named to the NFL's All-Time Team as a defensive tackle. Nomellini was inducted into the Pro Football Hall of Fame in 1969.

Position Defensive Tackle
Seasons 14 (1950–1963)
Born June 19, 1924, in Lucca, Italy

Steve Young

Steve Young came to San Francisco in 1987 to serve as Joe Montana's backup. An injury to Montana in 1991 allowed Young to show he could be a starting quarterback. He led the 49ers to the team's fifth Super Bowl championship in 1994. Young was named MVP.

Young topped all NFL quarterbacks in **passer rating** for six seasons, including four in a row from 1991 to 1994. Young retired in 1999 as the highest rated quarterback in NFL history. He was inducted into the Pro Football Hall of Fame in 2005.

Position Quarterback
Seasons 15 (1985–1999)
Born October 11, 1961, in Salt Lake City, Utah

Stars of Today

Today's 49ers team is made up of many young, talented players who have proven that they are among the best in the league.

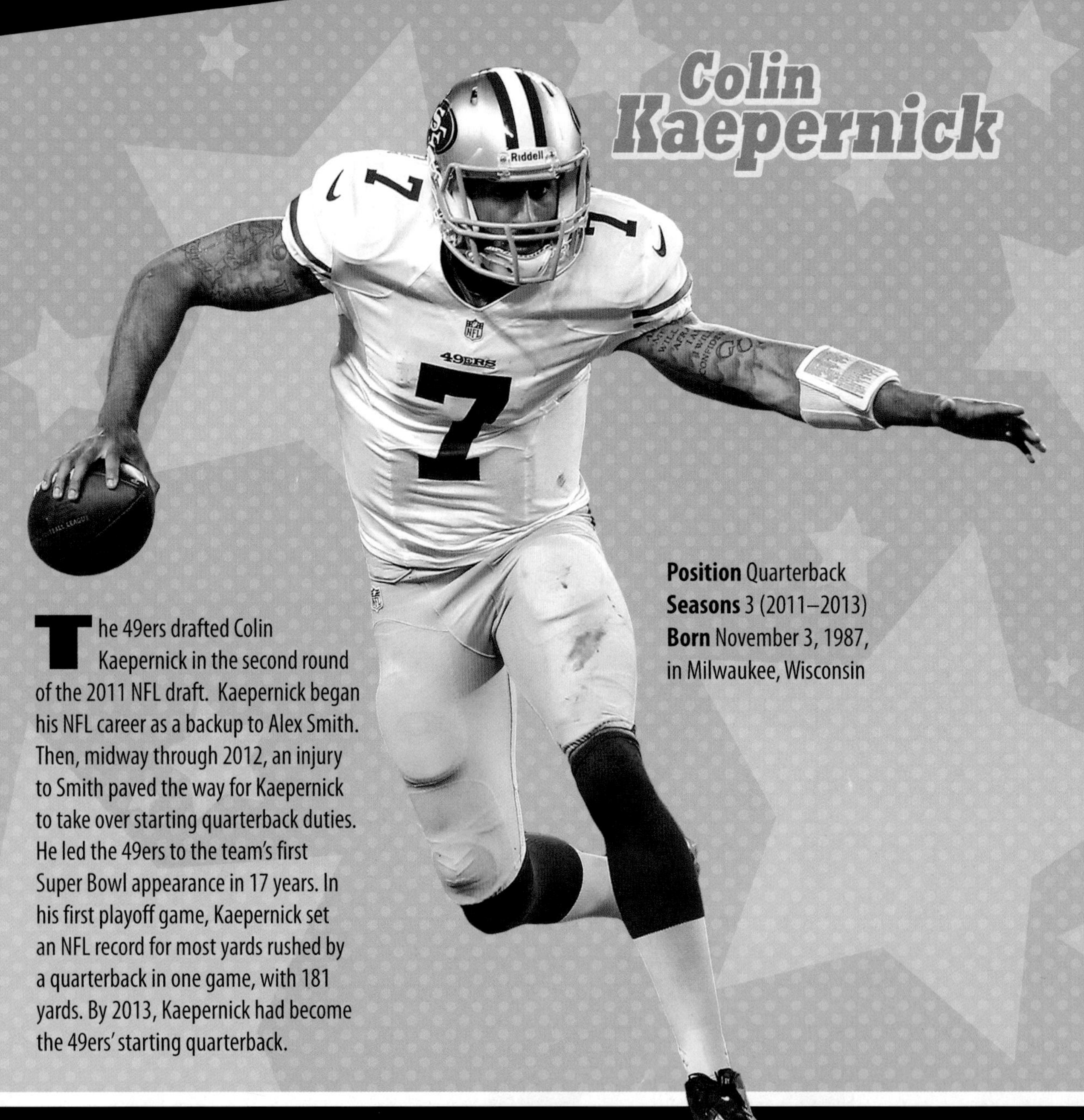

Colin Kaepernick

Position Quarterback
Seasons 3 (2011–2013)
Born November 3, 1987, in Milwaukee, Wisconsin

The 49ers drafted Colin Kaepernick in the second round of the 2011 NFL draft. Kaepernick began his NFL career as a backup to Alex Smith. Then, midway through 2012, an injury to Smith paved the way for Kaepernick to take over starting quarterback duties. He led the 49ers to the team's first Super Bowl appearance in 17 years. In his first playoff game, Kaepernick set an NFL record for most yards rushed by a quarterback in one game, with 181 yards. By 2013, Kaepernick had become the 49ers' starting quarterback.

Vernon Davis

Vernon Davis came into the NFL as one of the league's top prospects and highest-paid tight ends. After three seasons of poor performances and several injuries, Davis had a breakout season in 2009. He finished the year with 965 yards on 78 receptions. He also tied for the league lead in receiving touchdowns, with 13. Davis was named to the 2009 **Pro Bowl**, and he has been listed in the NFL Top 100 three times. In 2013, he was ranked 38th by fellow NFL players.

Position Tight End
Seasons 8 (2006–2013)
Born January 31, 1984, in Washington, D.C.

Patrick Willis

Many people believe Patrick Willis is the best inside linebacker in the NFL. After the 49ers selected him with the 11th overall pick in 2007, Willis quickly became a key part of the team. He finished his first season with a league-leading 174 tackles and was named Defensive Rookie of the Year. In six full seasons with the 49ers, Willis has been named to the Pro Bowl six times. He was also voted Linebacker of the Year three times by former NFL linebackers.

Position Linebacker
Seasons 7 (2007–2013)
Born January 25, 1985, in Bruceton, Tennessee

All-Time Records

19,247 All-time Receiving Yards

Jerry Rice holds nearly every receiving record for the 49ers. His records include most receiving touchdowns (176), most receiving yards in a season (1,848), and most receiving touchdowns in a season (22).

89.5 All-time Sacks

Defensive tackle Bryant Young holds the 49ers' team sack record. He played for the team from 1994 to 2007.

9,967 All-time Rushing Yards

Running back Frank Gore holds several 49ers rushing records, including most rushing yards. His other records include most rushing attempts (2,187) and most rushing touchdowns (60).

35,124 **All-time Passing Yards**

Joe Montana holds many of the 49ers passing records, including most all-time passing yards. He also holds the 49ers' record for most passing yards in a single game (476), which he set in 1990.

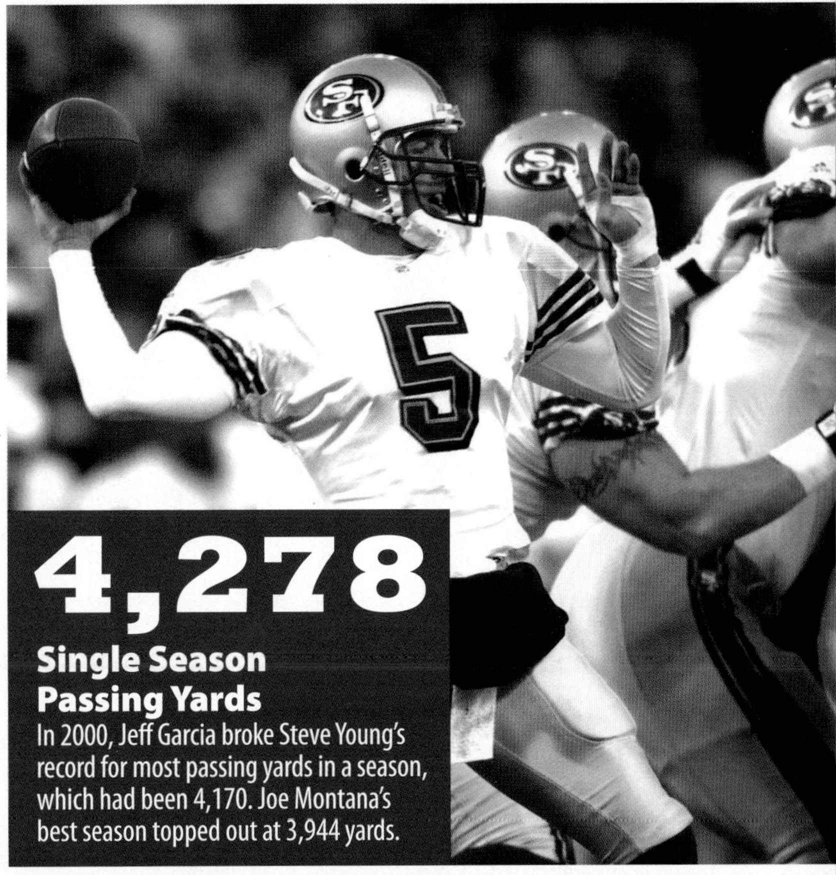

4,278

Single Season Passing Yards

In 2000, Jeff Garcia broke Steve Young's record for most passing yards in a season, which had been 4,170. Joe Montana's best season topped out at 3,944 yards.

Timeline

Throughout the team's history, the San Francisco 49ers have had many memorable events that have become defining moments for the team and its fans.

1942
Original San Francisco 49ers team owner, Tony Morabito, meets with NFL officials to propose a new team on the west coast. His request is turned down.

1944
After another failed attempt to join the NFL, Morabito agrees to enter a team in the new All-American Football Conference (AAFC).

August 24, 1946
The 49ers play their first game. They win 17-7 over the Los Angeles Dons in an **exhibition** game in San Diego.

1950
The 49ers play their first season in the NFL. They finish the season with three wins and nine losses.

October 27, 1957
Team founder and owner Tony Morabito dies of a heart attack during a 49ers game at Kezar Stadium. The 49ers went on to win their last three games.

The 49ers begin a string of 12 seasons without making the playoffs in 1958.

1940 1945 1950 1955 1960 1965

January 10, 1982
Down 27-21 with time running out in the NFC Championship, Joe Montana throws to Dwight Clark in the end zone. Clark jumps and makes "The Catch" on his fingertips to tie the game. The 49ers score the **extra point** for the win.

The Future
The San Francisco 49ers have one of the most talented young teams in the NFL. Under head coach Jim Harbaugh, the team has made a huge improvement in just a few years. After making it back to the playoffs in 2011 and to the Super Bowl in 2012, many people believe the 49ers are nearing their sixth Super Bowl championship.

1970
The 49ers win their first division title under head coach Dick Nolan and quarterback John Brodie.

The 49ers win back to back Super Bowls in 1988 and 1989.

2011
The 49ers hire former NFL quarterback Jim Harbaugh as head coach.

1970 | 1980 | 1990 | 2000 | 2010 | 2020

The 49ers enter a new era in 1979 with the additions of Joe Montana and coach Bill Walsh.

1994
Just one year after trading Joe Montana to the Kansas City Chiefs, quarterback Steve Young leads the 49ers to their fifth Super Bowl win.

February 3, 2013
Coach Jim Harbaugh and quarterback Colin Kaepernick lead the 49ers to the Super Bowl but lose 34-31 to the Baltimore Ravens.

1984
The 49ers complete one of the best seasons in NFL history. They finish the regular season with 15 wins and one loss. They then defeat the Miami Dolphins 38-16 to win their second Super Bowl.

1971
After winning their second straight division title, the 49ers lose to the Dallas Cowboys in the conference final for the second year in a row.

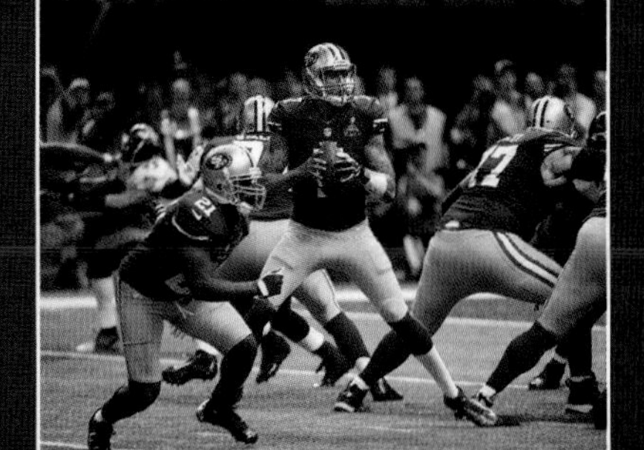

Write a Biography

Life Story

A person's life story can be the subject of a book. This kind of book is called a biography. Biographies often describe the lives of people who have achieved great success. These people may be alive today, or they may have lived many years ago. Reading a biography can help you learn more about a great person.

Get the Facts

Use this book, and research in the library and on the Internet, to find out more about your favorite 49er. Learn as much about this player as you can. What position does he play? What are his statistics in important categories? Has he set any records? Also, be sure to write down key events in the person's life. What was his childhood like? What has he accomplished off the field? Is there anything else that makes this person special or unusual?

Use the Concept Web

A concept web is a useful research tool. Read the questions in the concept web on the following page. Answer the questions in your notebook. Your answers will help you write a biography.

Concept Web

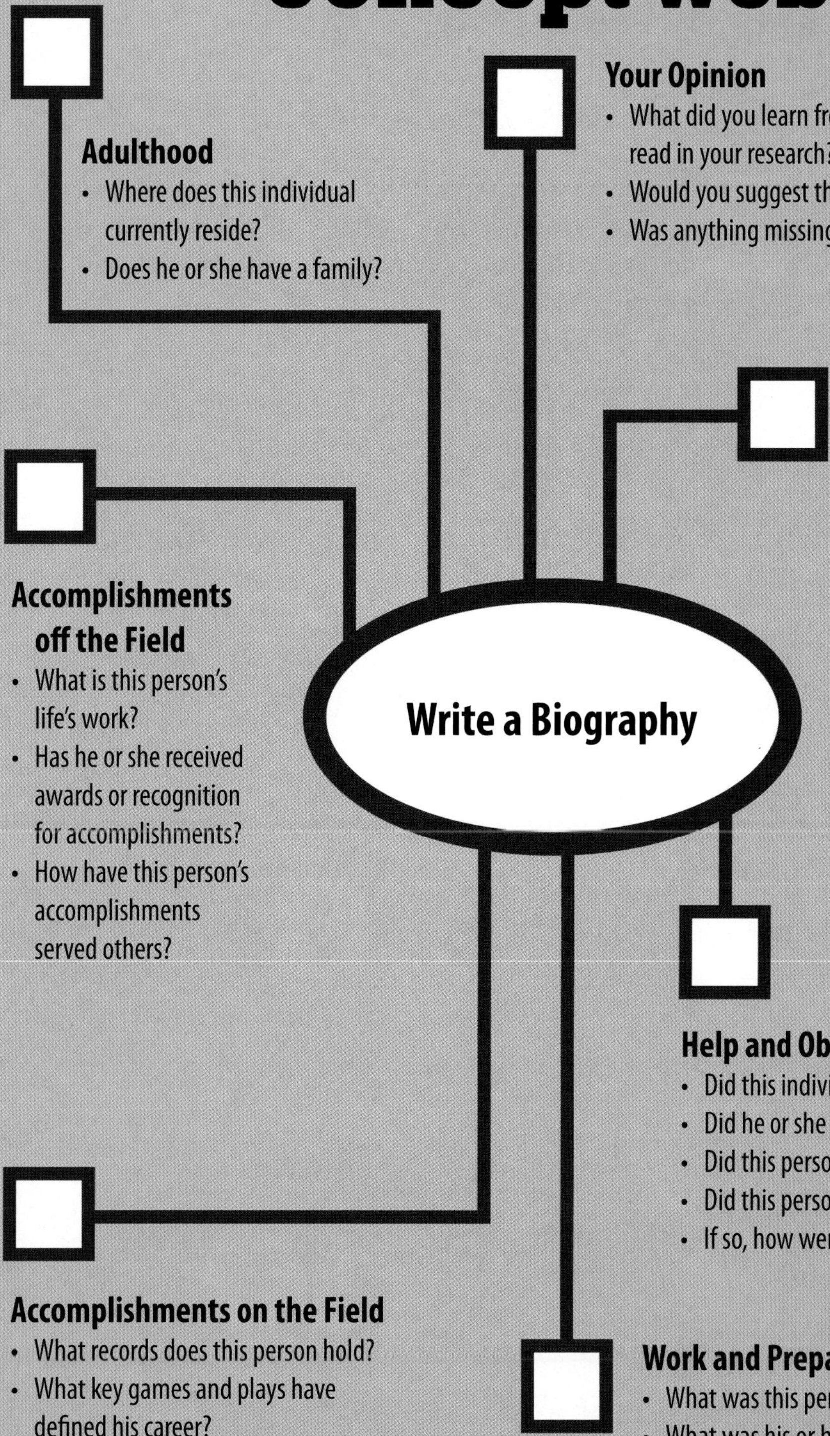

Adulthood
- Where does this individual currently reside?
- Does he or she have a family?

Your Opinion
- What did you learn from the books you read in your research?
- Would you suggest these books to others?
- Was anything missing from these books?

Childhood
- Where and when was this person born?
- Describe his or her parents, siblings, and friends.
- Did this person grow up in unusual circumstances?

Accomplishments off the Field
- What is this person's life's work?
- Has he or she received awards or recognition for accomplishments?
- How have this person's accomplishments served others?

Write a Biography

Help and Obstacles
- Did this individual have a positive attitude?
- Did he or she receive help from others?
- Did this person have a mentor?
- Did this person face any hardships?
- If so, how were the hardships overcome?

Accomplishments on the Field
- What records does this person hold?
- What key games and plays have defined his career?
- What are his stats in categories important to his position?

Work and Preparation
- What was this person's education?
- What was his or her work experience?
- How does this person work; what is the process he or she uses?

Trivia Time

Take this quiz to test your knowledge of the San Francisco 49ers. The answers are printed upside-down under each question.

1 How many Super Bowl championships have the 49ers won? In which years did they win?

A. Five: 1981, 1984, 1988, 1989, and 1994

2 What is the style of offense that came to define the 49ers during the team's run of success in the 1980s and early 1990s?

A. The West Coast offense, which focused on short, accurate passes

3 Who is the 49ers' all-time leader in almost every receiving category?

A. Jerry Rice

4 Who made "The Catch" that sent the 49ers to their first ever Super Bowl championship?

A. Dwight Clark

5 Which 49ers' quarterback holds the all-time team record for passing yards?

A. Joe Montana

6 Which 49ers' coach holds the record for having the highest winning percentage during his time in San Francisco?

A. George Seifert

7 Which league did the San Francisco 49ers play in from 1946 to 1949?

A. The All-American Football Conference (AAFC)

8 Who is the 49ers' all-time rushing leader?

A. Frank Gore

9 Which current 49ers' linebacker holds the team record for most sacks in one season?

A. Aldon Smith

10 What is the name of the 49ers' team mascot?

A. Sourdough Sam

Key Words

All-American: a player, usually in high school or college, judged to be the best in each position of a sport

All-Pro: an NFL player judged to be the best in his position for a given season

dynasties: teams that win a series of championships in a short period of time

exhibition: a game played outside of the regular season schedule that does not affect the ranking of either team

extra point: an attempt awarded after each touchdown scored that allows the offensive team to kick the ball through the goalposts for an extra point

logo: a symbol that stands for a team or organization

most valuable player (MVP): the player judged to be most valuable to his team's success

passer rating: a rating given to quarterbacks that tries to measure how well they perform on the field

Pro Bowl: the annual all-star game for NFL players, pitting the best players in the National Football Conference against the best players in the American Football Conference

Super Bowl: the NFL's annual championship game between the winning team from the NFC and the winning team from the AFC

winning percentage: the number of games won divided by the total number of games played; a coach with 7 wins in 10 games would have a winning percentage of 70 percent

Index

Log on to www.av2books.com

AV² by Weigl brings you media enhanced books that support active learning. Go to www.av2books.com, and enter the special code found on page 2 of this book. You will gain access to enriched and enhanced content that supplements and complements this book. Content includes video, audio, weblinks, quizzes, a slide show, and activities.

AV² Online Navigation

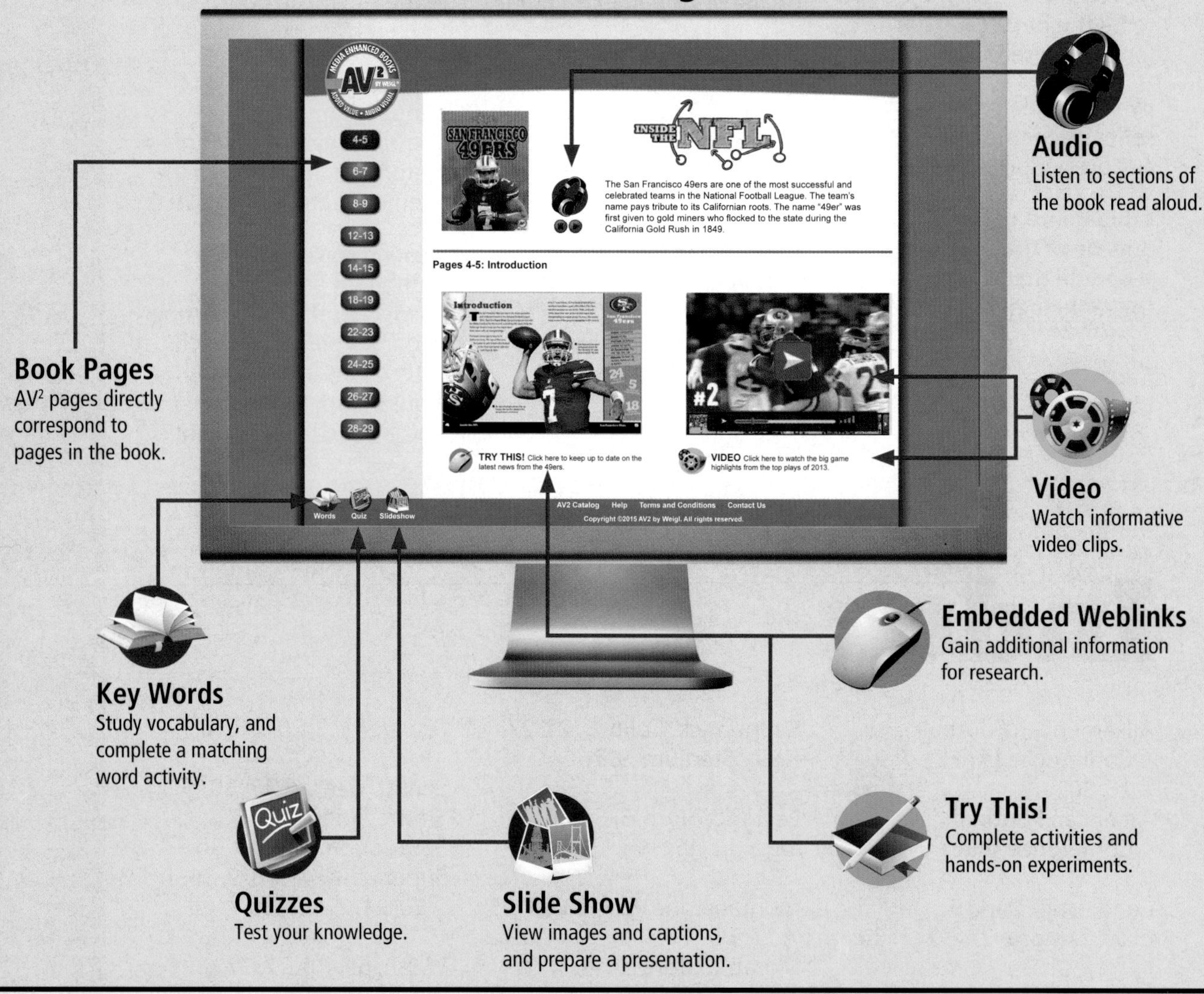

AV² was built to bridge the gap between print and digital. We encourage you to tell us what you like and what you want to see in the future.

Sign up to be an AV² Ambassador at www.av2books.com/ambassador.

Due to the dynamic nature of the Internet, some of the URLs and activities provided as part of AV² by Weigl may have changed or ceased to exist. AV² by Weigl accepts no responsibility for any such changes. All media enhanced books are regularly monitored to update addresses and sites in a timely manner. Contact AV² by Weigl at 1-866-649-3445 or av2books@weigl.com with any questions, comments, or feedback.